SIGNAL
FIRES

BY CHRISTOPHER DEWDNEY

POETRY

Golders Green 1971
A Palaeozoic Geology of London, Ontario 1973
Fovea Centralis 1975
Alter Sublime 1980
Predators of the Adoration 1983
Permugenesis 1987
The Radiant Inventory 1988
Demon Pond 1994
Signal Fires 2000

NON-FICTION

The Immaculate Perception 1986
The Secular Grail 1993
Last Flesh 1998

SIGNAL
FIRES

Christopher Dewdney

M&S

Canadian Cataloguing in Publication Data

Dewdney, Christopher, 1951-
  Signal fires

Poems.
ISBN 0-7710-2739-7

I. Title.

PS8557.E846S53 2000 C811'.54 C00-930402-9
PR9199.3.D48S53 2000

We acknowledge the financial support of the Government of Canada through the Book Publishing Industry Development Program for our publishing activities. We further acknowledge the support of the Canada Council for the Arts and the Ontario Arts Council for our publishing program.

Typeset in Sabon by M&S, Toronto
Printed and bound in Canada

McClelland & Stewart Inc.
The Canadian Publishers
481 University Avenue
Toronto, Ontario
M5G 2E9

1 2 3 4 5   04 03 02 01 00

CONTENTS

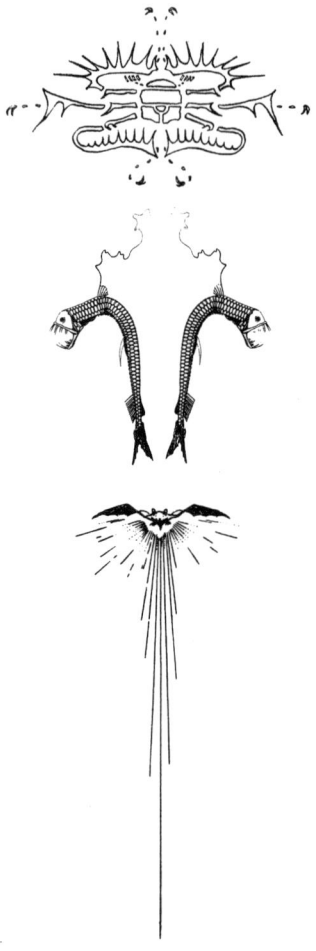

CONCORDAT PROVISO ASCENDANT

BOOK III

A Natural History of Southwestern Ontario

David Heath, an English teacher at Xenia High School in Xenia, Ohio, was conducting an after-school drama class on an unusually hot June afternoon. Around 4:25 a student burst into the drama workshop, which was located in the school auditorium, and announced that a tornado was approaching.

"I came very close to telling everyone to forget it and to go through the dance number we were rehearsing again. Instead I jumped off the stage and told everyone to follow me so we could get a good view of the tornado. I imagined a funnel cloud in the sky that we could look at and then return to rehearsing. When we arrived at the front doors to the school we were astonished to see a viciously twisting column less than two hundred yards away. Then, cars parked in front of the school began to bounce around. It was beyond belief. Someone said we'd better take cover, so we all ran towards the centre hall of the school. The lights went out just before we turned the corner and crouched against the walls on both sides of the corridor.

"Then the tornado struck. The weird thing was the sound of it, like the clattering of a thousand sets of Venetian blinds, along with tremendous crashing and grating sounds. When I opened my eyes a couple of times I saw large pieces of dirt and wood flying horizontally down the corridor. Then, for a moment, the wind stopped. One of the boys stood up, but I yelled at him to

get down. Then the wind struck again with seemingly greater force. We were all hit with dirt, broken glass, mud, wood, heaven knows what else. I was still picking glass out of my scalp two days later. Finally it stopped, and there was total silence.

"When we stood up it was lighter than usual, and I looked up and noticed that the roof was entirely missing. Later we found out the ceiling of the auditorium had collapsed and that a school bus lay upside down on the stage where we had been rehearsing."

S he is beyond you now. Her piscine features embryonic & dissipated with wisdom. Her nakedness possessed each time a seething harlequin of erectile sequins. Her lips aching with honey. The sky darkening with dreams.

There is a language to predicate the adoration.

And the water, its essence an alarming grace unfolding past the edge of your control. Breeding miraculous witness. Command spillover. Trembling mica electron thunder. Distant blue spruce shimmer vaguely, their translucent pagodas rising like glass temples in the dusk. The ammonoid's nacreous lustre, iridescent stage lights in a Cretaceous theatre. Slow-motion August trees, the Huron clay bluffs blue in the lake haze & at night the stars rain glittering onto the beach. Pyritized mother of pearl a refraction so ancient the dreams are blackened. This most Devonian of raptures. A vowel away from the discrete crystals wherein her rude beauty gives way to angels. As the planet turns into the photon irradiation of dawn. Our debt to the truth.

Beneath the lake a room. The water electric. The smallest ripple transmitted undiminished through the whole. For its membrane is the progenitor of the cellular envelope, budding cauldrons at the base of the falls. It is living. It whispers & moans a thousand voices within the rapids. It is the medium of choice for internal predators.

Day lilies waxen cups of orange & red conspiring under
the late afternoon sun. Dazzling cellular lattice.
Rattlesnake Point.

Dusty milkweeds at the roadside. Summer cricket fields
phasing a pointillistic audio plane. Waves of wind
transparent molasses in the leaves. Insect voyeurs.

It is night and there is a yearning in the wind. Your
heart a dusky corporeal fragrance streaming into the
stars. In the moonlight you can see the underwater
trees. Devonian ocean floor commands the summer
sky a fossil sea. Spicebush, oak & sassafras. The
mouth of the Ausable. Blue evening dunes of the Pinery.
This sunrise a coral fire through the hardwood
crowns. Leafless spring forest glowing tide against
the sun-fissured escarpment. Incremental heat of the
vernal arc high over Collingwood.

Specific mist of August, pink & gold. A morning light
all day. The forest shade almost colloidal, darkening
under the looming thunderheads. Lilacs. Nicotinia. A
penetrating dampness, limp clothes & paper, the subway
floors sweat under her sandals. Gracile her slim body.
Gamelan the thrill of her hands. A proton decay
detection chamber under the south shore of Erie. Her
toes an almost Fibonacci sequence, her lips tasting of
unknown cities. Rain shimmers in the Zildjian forest. A
bat flying through Allen Gardens. Glass membrane
ruptured into the June night sky, itself an infernal
mosaic of irregular cobalt tiles, prismatic sparks at their

4

interstices. Her sex flushed by the fire lithe under the trees. Words unable me to speak to you. There is a path for you hear if you see it. She was paradise renewed a tangible & immaculate vision. Blue the colour of opium once in a dream.

Awkward mammalian blossoms in cool sunlight the memory of a childhood not our own. Occidental blue of April afternoons, distant north an aerial clarion in the heavens. As if the sky would quicken and reveal another scale of perspective, a giant immanence of dreams born in wordless childhood musings. The April plainness of building materials on cold grey afternoons. Provisional shelter. At night the glistening celestial machinery. Sky deepening with stars, crescent of the new moon just setting above the glow of sunset. Concrete technical reality. There is a heraldry in creation unseen. Stony morning brook, sparkling water beads the optical distillation of the previous night's stars. Star dew. The rain we pray for. Recognition in the May foliage, secret arboreal house of dreams & wind. Star corridors. The axis insatiable. Labialithe.

A temporal music, each successive note justified only by its predecessor. Such subtle harmony that the edge of dissonance suspends the speed of beauty. Grey and gold escarpment the October rain. Let them all see it. May night a reality of precise darkness gushing the wildest hot metals into her red shift depths. Bronze rivers sinuous with age. Boreal rawness of early June foliage. Huron palisade the plateau forest of the Escarpment. A single firefly, portentous intermittent star wending silently through dim canyons of spruce. This meandering green ember insinuates the solid obsidian glass night, a supernumerary planet adding its strange light to the stars. Unearthly machinery of the forest darkness. Nightshade. Low frequency rumble of the planetary surface. The night before the day after. Summer sun a cool furnace in the furthest depths of the moon. The avenues we drive home on. Solstice moon waxing pale in the afternoon sky. Evergreen. Chlorophyll & haemoglobin. Red Haven. The music frightening & joyous. I have the vehicle to take you there, its gleaming fuselage a landscape foreshortened by velocity.

Take command of the senses. You are all that you see. Cardinal in the redbud. The lake milky blue green under the purple sky of an approaching electrical storm. Something ironic in you which is not fully formed. This moment gone too far. Delirium in the summer wind. Midnight cicada. Proliferation of crickets. The horizon a window of impossible perspective, multi-layered stratus & cumulonimbus. A path the least resistance.

Cap & talus of the Escarpment diminishing into perspective haze at our sides. Grimsby ravine an irresistible river of gravity, sensual cushion over the unwavering creek. Her abdomen pale cream curdled with muscles. Her power a private delight arched & supple. Her thrall of nakedness. Pseudoscorpions under shoes on the landing. Fruitflies. Peaches. October moon a glaucous eye through altostratus. A life refined to one unbearable moment. Love a semantics you invent between. Her touch a thrilling cellular wind racing through my nervous system. This wet skin & sweet absence. The mild labile hysteria of gulls.

Lustful engine of summer metal quickening within the late March railway soil. Hot shaft of the vernal axis naked under bare sumac branches. Her breath exquisite musk reminiscent of the osmoderma. Elora Gorge, summer reptile sunbanks the cool morning cedar forest aloft on each side. Ocular water sliding lager beneath quick ledges. Limestone caves. There is an ineffable music that lingers in the charged air over the rapids. A single note triggers intangible symphonies, their strange harmonies blend into the fabric of all sound.

Late night rhapsody of the ecliptic, ultramarine spangled with planets. The looming almost frightening wisdom of children. The still city a crystal lattice dreaming under the bright shoals of Lake Iroquois. Our orgasm an embodied mutual description. River mist pungent malt of liquid leaves. Branches, roots, boulders & niches, the landscape proffers itself for our progress on the slopes. Seminal blue electric glow within the waterfall. Demerara floor of the cedar forest striped with sun. Limestone terraces mark the descent of an ancestral river. Ramparts encased in cedarn foliage, a photon greenhouse evanescent in July heat. Each bank of the gorge an interior unknowable to the other.

Darkness comes early in the valley, twisting along the paths like warm river wind, a corporeal zephyr. Time skewed with silence in the chiming afternoon. An autumn indistinguishable from morning proceeding like no other. The gorge sweats above the white heat of the rapids. Cedar, hemlock, white pine & birch. Elm & ash beyond. Gorge patrol. Dry riverbed of twilight & night in the cedar forest, fragrant darkness spills down the shallow fossil valley.

Toronto interglacial overcast. A temperate, deciduous freshwater marine light. Metal at high speed. White clay bluffs & summer interiors burgundy & pale dusty green. Purple stone. Wood smoke and evening mist the water pellucid jelly. Moiré of ripples an inverse solution to the equation of shoreline. The wind a sudden aerial

rapids in the leaves. This nightriver, gentle grade &
bowl & groove.

Faintly pungent, acrid limestone river rank from trickle
falls luxurious with moss. Still grace the rainforest mist
intermittent showers retained by the canopy released.
Mercurial chipmunks, warm tubular & insistent, their
lingering stripes. Blue ash. The forest roots a semiology
we just barely comprehend. I have the music to take
you there, its gleaming fuselage just beyond the curve of
this hill. Drone of cicadas adorning the beech temple,
serpentine roots burst the foundation stones.
Underwater shelves of limestone. Salamanders moist
beneath dry forest rocks. Dolomite gleaming with
crystals, calcite vugs within. Bracken. Quantum flight
of a hoverfly. Still, heavy air, thunder low in the
distance. Elastic twang of a bullfrog locates the
shallows. The night gorge pulsing with fireflies,
moonlight on waves. Trembling mica electron thunder
an underground city.

She is liquid darkness occult with desire. Scattered curls of corrugated steel litter the floor of an abandoned airplane hangar. The naked air electric we unite glistening in the light from giant atmospheric machines rising above the horizon. The sky filled with sound, furious insistent joy as she cries, aching chorus of electroluminescent orgasm. Heat-bleached August fields. Cool green lawns under humid tree caverns. Lambton forest a cool sensual intuition, earthen paths packed & powdered. Night perfume of the magnolia blossoms drifting through the limestone trestles under the railway bridge. Cicada shimmer in the late summer trees. Storm flooded city streets and aromatic twigs. Her incendiary hands stoke the September heatwave, a single katydid rasping from the silver maple at midnight. In the humid wind magnified leaf shadows enact a restless cinema under the backyard floodlight. Wild grapes purple on the vine. Particulate smoky blue haze of hot October afternoons. Indian summer in the Berkshires. Manhattan. Wild rhododendrons of the Hudson valley.

Becoming myself, I have become someone else. My adoration the natural fulfilment of her sacral narcissism. She is Eros displayed. Lank salience of her thighs as she consumes me. She drew a shade of stratus. Chunks of stone erode into Mayan friezes. Gold scarabs at Clark Point. She won't stop until you've come unnaturally again and again. Creek newts frankly relaxed in the sandy aquarium delta foliage. An otter near the forks of the Ervin and Grand. Cedar roots dowsing Silurian strata. Prodigious acrobatics of cliff swallows. She is here now. Her face a dark lantern blossoming in the twilight. Every path the most expedient solution of opposite destinations. She lies down amongst the ferns. Manitoulin cecropias. A flute lost in the sound of rapids.

Scarab grubs harboured in scrub oaks. We merge in the windy forest, in the rushing neo-silence of a hot August wind, in the mute aqueous clamour of leaves under the wild hush of the forest. Our clothes sullen layers of skin. Our giant bodies' moist electric surfaces continuous with the forest. Close upon us now this afternoon an atmosphere of flesh. The smell of rain on the wind. August hypnotized in cool depths of the lake. Mudpuppy. Hellbender. September heatwave stone temple haze along the beach distant signal fires glimmering orange. Her water broke the slow fall of evening leaves, waves of silver green above human creatures coupling wondrous beneath. Chlorophyll mist. The sky ringing with our music.

Our path a dark sweetness, musky tribute to your surrender. Your face miraculous stone sweating in the August heat. The sky a dream of cirrus & aquamarine, purple silhouettes of distant airplanes descending into the edge of night. High evening this secret joyous darkness internally illuminated by a fossil sun. Night windows of a large home near the river. In the cool dark of the basement nocturnal children interlock within the necessities of desire. Their faces animal flowers insensate with beauty. Tropical leaf theatre under stadium lights.

The stars through hot leaves our bodies dusted with forest & surely engaged by a slender path. Indistinct in twilight we rub ourselves with dirt & slide mucous pink into each other again and again, the merging earth our union & we ache for the river music, a blanket of silence. Its impassive interior a mute concourse. Night eyes. We are intruders in our own house, incandescent lights a peripheral flicker our bodies smudged with soil. Our reflection in the picture window, night trees behind. You come rubbing against me we come androgynous we come as two boys & then as two women. A cistern of rainwater in the cellar. A rainbarrel in the garden & in the stream our bodies indissoluble within the warm river currents there. Gradual accumulation of insects at the porch light, a glittering raiment. Our bodies quick & light through the night air. Dusty pink evening at the botanical gardens. Neural storms in her pupils. A magnetic field suddenly explicit around two trees as a flock of birds erupting from one is sucked into another. Avian prominence the lines of force. There are salamanders nearby.

G othic geometry of the lycopod forest. The axis of symmetry explicit in the angular lattice of fern canopy. Rustling flight of a giant dragonfly. Cellophane wings glint in the Carboniferous sunlight, a vanishing, airy chain of after-images. The humidity of the gorge forest higher than the surrounding area. A world millions of years in the past. Snake Doctor, helicopter, red Doppler Shift. My camp a rainforest vigil here at the transition zone. The camouflaged wings of the moth are pure representation. A path is an inter-species collaboration. Distant rumble of thunder older even than the shark. Iridescent blue scarab deep within the petals of a rose.

Watersnakes bask on sunny riverbanks. Ion shadow of the thunderhead hovering sightless over this forest a charmed garden. Fabric of reality parting slightly just before lightning. Swimming naked in the warm night river. Umbilical tornado. Copper oxide & limestone chambers. Lynx rampant on a field sable. The crown of night. The margin of heaven and earth blurred this evening. Moonrise.

The water is continuous music manifesting the bias of the valley. Adolescents shimmer in the corruption of self-consciousness, their limbs bronze & gold under the summer sun. The sunlight pale stained-glass green, the forest a cathedral, its floor studded with remains of ancient temples dedicated to unknown gods. Elora Gorge an erogenous wound in the surface of the limestone. Dusky salamanders, translucent licorice speckled with silver. There is a landscape that

corresponds to each station of the heart, a geography
for every phase of our lives.

The Elora Gorge is a rift valley in time, an amphitheatre
of cedar & limestone. Hot green twilight of the forest
depths. Decaying Hindu temples, each built on the
crumbling summit of its predecessor. Roots & vines
form a twisted webbing over limestone walls. Umbrella
magnolias & blue ash. Giant swallowtail butterfly
momentary cadmium in the shadowy interior of the
forest. Water wrestling with rocks in the depths of
the rapids. The gorge air still & heavy, the sky misting
over into a featureless bright grey haze, maximum
heat of early evening. Distant thunder. Nighthawks,
crickets, bats & raccoons, wild continuum into the
centres of the Great Lake cities.

K arst topography. Bright hypnotic splendour of the solstice noon. A dragonfly lands on her shoulder, its rainbow wings glittering in the June sunlight. Endless summer night of the high Arctic Eocene. Her ancestral Devonian arms sinister. Giant catalpa trees bear signal standards of white blossoms, profound and lucid in the cloudless solar morning. On still nights their fragrance cascades in sweet penumbras, nocturnal skirts of perfume. Limestone trestles of the railway bridge are erotic monuments in the television foliage of an industrial age summer. Barberry blossoms' spermy pungency on hot June nights. Cartilaginous sex. Grey diffuse light of memory, a sensualizing texture irrupting & sweetening everything with cosmic nostalgia for the moment. Each second a prodigal return, reality re-corporealized with recognition.

Fess engrailed. Mammatocumulus illuminated from beneath by the setting sun. Night hardwood on the summer campus, Corinthian columns ascend through successive tiers of concentric leaf mobiles, deciduous candelabra. Their outlines slowly ripple in the hallucinogenic mist of the nocturnal forest, indiscernible from the veritable animation of the night wind. Delicate wallpaper clouds approach the full moon in this cinema blue night. The forest is a room we dissipate into, particularize. Involute masters of uncertain dimensions.

Muscular black night wind dusty with stars. Blowing clear & hot from the boreal summer. The faint brown band of skin around the middle of my cock. Jerusalem

wind through northern valleys, dark mountains stir
within the alchemical night, giant sensual gods sculpted
in basalt. Desert wind a thousand years old and clear as
deuterium pools, a wind blowing empty through our
hearts, their mysterious longing. A wind that pulls us
wordless from our bodies, the rushing final wind. The
historical wind erotic & spiritual, stone deities coupling
on the walls of jungle temples. Eocene nachtmusik.

So fair our green. Testicular sacs of the oriole nest,
winged persimmons in her green vigilance. The
honeysuckle's buzzing insect aura. Sun sporadically
through hazy cumulus clouds, the lake impenetrable
with mist. Stiff, incremental surge of growing trees.
Forest light is the perpetual, internal twilight of dreams.
I am the fisher king of my unconscious. Root cascades
on rocks, gnarled retainers for terraced humus
waterfalls, the re-enactment of a fossil rapids.
Delightfully uneven terrain. Forest rocks luminous with
condensation, green antler-velvet congealed into stone.
The clamour of the storm lags in noisy streams.

Distant apartment complexes become moody empires of light, subdued orange constellations in the twilight haze. Revelation of the rainy day. Late night resurrection of a forgotten love, a vanished civilization where the waning moon is the accusational eye of a discarded lover. Metaphysics in dusty light on the trunks of the Norway spruce, cicada husks at their bases. Windbreak colonnade. Love's absence is love still, the heart a celestial wound. August a certain Aegean light through us all. The beach a commotion of light and waves, cries of gulls and children blend in the wind. Honeysuckle vines redolent of evening, a dusky corona of ruby throats. Surprising articulation of children's backs, their advanced hominid wisdom. Wild cherry gum on raw copper. The dull gleam of tin roofs. Field of hydroelectric power flickering in the darkness at the lake bottom.

She is delightfully augmented. In the distance vandals break windows in a deserted factory, disembodied locus of fear. Meander. She walks almost laboriously around her endowments, a libidinous & circuitous elegance. She is crippled with sex, ripe fruit on a slender bough. Resume the broken discourse of the gods. Quick vertigo of lust. The Milky Way wheeling on the axis of an immense black hole through abandoned zodiacs in the mysterious depths of an intergalactic summer night. A continuous indoor atmosphere extends uniform & infinite in all directions.

Long Tooth

We are fire monkeys,
soft itchy hunters with
warm stingers sheathed in fur.
We are skinny apes
who mime both hunter and prey, whose
kindness lies in pain, whose
sacrificial instructions are the singular
charity of our deathly logic.

We are electric apes
who hunt our own children
to teach them the higher way,
the path that sharpens
claws and teeth,
the path within
they must clear
for themselves.

We are weary hunters,
our bloody mammalian inheritance
cast in stars and dreams and words.
We are thin, famished poachers waiting
at the edge of the world. We are pedagogical
savages listening for the footfalls
of our students, apprentices
to be sacrificed in our jaws,
honed to the lessons of our teeth,
the whistling shape of our skulls.

We are smart worms
who eat our way
into the carcasses of animals, then
rise up in malefic parody,
grotesque marionettes,
ripped and skinned and dyed.
we gnaw within, fashion
lethal technologies from skeletons and
slaughter others with their own bones, worked malign
into deadly revision of tooth and claw.

Tooth and claw improved,
tooth and claw in monstrous service,
the carnivorous disarticulation of
beasts, our monkey fetish
unsheathing still more bones
from their muscled red pockets.

We are fire monkeys.
The long tooth
betrays us.

KILLBEAR

The last summer moon
high over the trees,
the forest splashed piebald
with moonlight.
Tristan dreaming
in the tent beneath motionless leaves.

In the moonlight
our camp shows clearly.
Tent under the tarpaulin,
wash basin, water jugs,
seats improvised around the smouldering fire.
Towels and bathing suits
on a sway-backed line.
Wilderness home.
This moment forever,
and never again.
Tonight our dreams rise
to the second world
above this lunar checkerboard.
Tomorrow
the vortex
of the city.

Gravid Lux

for Barbara in Antigua

Tonight the Antillean sky is unnaturally clear,
the moon's faint, perennial halo is gone.
South of Orion's sword the tropic stars
spangle a trail to the equator.
By the lagoon, coconut palms
rustle and slide their leathery wings.
Beyond the beach,
a faint susurrus of waves
breaking on the crest
of the reef.

The warm trade wind is stronger
on the hill above the bay.
It moans in power lines and the screens
of houses near the road. It whistles
through the shutters of our hotel room where
ceiling fans slice the ocean air.
Their bleak, electric hum a counterpoint
to the low-grade bliss
of dreaming in the tropics.

Under the thraldom of our idyll,
in the mute cosmic witness of this night.
there is a poignance,
as if such mildness could purge the north,
climate of steel and asphalt.

By the lagoon,
in the buttress forest of the mangrove,
a large white crab delicately stilts
over the mud flats. We
are dream factories, underwater gardens
hang in our heads.

The trade wind is filled with mad lovers
while in northern darkness
pale fields sleep
under the red wings
of winter.

Without Him

A eulogy for Bob Gowdy

To come to an end, finally
exhausted by the effort
to remain in the world.
Not a relief to die.
Numb flesh, so abandoned in death.

No relief to die in the night, to abandon
your work, what
you would have finished.
Not the life work, but the framing
of wood and steel and glass.
The table you were building
at Balsam Lake.

Towards the end you resembled
a Mayan deity, your eyes huge,
alert, crystalline and shining
in your spectral face.
You became Ah Pook, the skeleton god of death,
your head illuminated from within,
like a carved quartz skull.
A certainty there,
terrible and clear.

To say goodbye
to nights by the water,
to the house you built, to your children's

children. To say goodbye to all this,
more than goodbye.
So much more than goodbye.
And to come to the end, alone
where none can follow.

And now these
eulogies. Maybe we've got it wrong.
Maybe *that* is death,
getting it wrong,
while the dead
wane into fiction
and we, the living, carry off bits,
like ants, a piecemeal dispersion.

But above it all
caught some notes of your music
the other day,
sketches you finished
the week before you died.

Let what you made
scatter into the world.
It never regretted
a minute of you.

On the Beach

I

That afternoon we walked
along the beach, you
turned to me,
the sun in your hair,
with your eyes saying goodbye, forever
goodbye. Abandoned. The wind
flickered through your hair, filled
the sails of an armada of desertion.
You told me it was the wind
not our will
that moved the world,
though your eyes were empty.

That day, above all the days before,
the beach rang with the commotion
of waves & wind, the heat of the sun.
Through the October chill it lingered.

The emptiness you spilled then
opened the afternoon, arched it
higher than blue could possibly arch
so the stars came out.
Though our sad euphoria
could not fuel such stars as these.

And the beach spread beneath us,
a white expanse, winged, as if

harpsichords played invisible in the air,
as if we walked on microscopic cobble
laid by the waves.

II

Later, alone in the evening,
after the wind had died and the sun
had set, I found
our afternoon steps and saw
that our footprints, like all footprints,
were blind.

Night's machinery was concealed
behind the blue-violet eastern sky.
There was a presentiment of moonlight,
a silver mist rising behind the dunes.
the calm evening light, a lucidity
beyond loneliness, loneliness
beyond consolation. I
remembered the day, the wind,
the way you turned to me,
the sun in your eyes,
and the hollow
of the sky, receding
like ice.

III

Outside this country house
November weeds are sparkling
with hoarfrost in starlight.

I have turned off the lamps
to see the ornate fields, the
occult splendour of an evening
only I will ever know. The quick, strange music
of a winter's night. This
beauty unknowable,
unspeakable. Through
my mind a wind blows
along an October beach.

IV

Hot wind through the summer fields,
a thrill that brushes
lovers entwined like ciphers in relic barns,
that bends dusty milkweed beside
cottage lanes. The inexorable
succession of grace, of love,
if only secured by great sadness, is
love's paradox. Those we cannot bear to leave
we must leave, those
we most adore we must abandon
to the stars – who dare
to burn unique
in the darkness.

V

That day on the beach, our only reunion,
a nation in diaspora.
Now we wait, listening

to the heart of our silence,
to ice forming in the moonlight.

VI

If I fall into my life,
if I fall back into my life, if
all the nights I was afraid, alone,
rose in great white rings of fear,
would love unravel like broken art,
in the irresistible,
unwavering bliss of an understanding
beyond comprehension? Would this evening return
again and again, stand
outside time and inhabit the moment
tragic in transitory beauty?

Then the clouds, frozen in memory, *would* shift,
the October beach be animate once again.

The thrust of time
its sheer rocketry
carries us far beyond that day,
and yet to be propelled
so effortlessly is splendid.

VII

Now time
has found the edge of our footsteps
and we are in the last place, our life

reduced to a series of spiral chambers,
containing each of our ages,
enclosed in the next, each
surrounded by darkness,
and in each a silence, a conversation
interrupted by our absence.
Within your greed for my soul
I watch the night arrive
through the evening
of the day you left.

Desert Angel

The door of the desert has opened,
skeletons of words
tumble in the frozen wind like dead leaves.
I have awakened
from the dream of meaning
into the implacable narcissism
of the word.
For within words is the progeny of words.
and I am caught in their honey.

In the transparent desert air
the angel appeared, flattened
against a dividend of reality so temporal,
so variegated, she was consumed
by the blank empire
of its shadows. She shone,
dustily iridescent in the
waning light of the setting sun
and I saw the ghosts of words,
painful, beautiful,
pluck her sides
like kites.

Now, within the fossil dance of words,
when letters are hung like insects
in mind's amber, I sing
this dusty kingdom of Braille,
while the skeletons of words,

the shadows of shadows
intone our empty names
across the dusty plain.

TIME WIND

BOOK IV

A NATURAL HISTORY OF
SOUTHWESTERN ONTARIO

*"About 9:15 in the evening we heard a loud roaring sound
southwest of the house which we believed to be an advancing
tornado. We went immediately into our storm cellar, an under-
ground dugout. I was the last one of the family to enter the
cellar – I had just closed the door, and was preparing to secure
it with a logging chain, when the tornado struck. The door
burst from its hinges and the chain was ripped out of my hand.
Both went sailing into the wide open spaces. It became very
dark as the edge of the tornado went over but inside the vortex
there was considerable illumination. I am sure I could see up to
a height of five hundred feet or more. The colour of this light
was a purplish pink, like the light that comes from brush dis-
charge of static electricity. I saw parts of our house, the out-
buildings, and a large tree carried into the already debris-filled
vortex. I ducked down into the dugout before the other side of
the tornado went over us."*

Mr. J.P. Molen
Weather Bureau Meteorologist
Hunt County, Texas
August 8, 1912.

C oal forest of the Carboniferous delta swamps. Lepidodendron trees, their anthracite trunks embossed with spirals of interlocking diamond leaf-scars. Exquisite fusain sceptres. Snakes and ladders. The river current quickens as it nears the falls. Elastic water pulled viscous over the lip. Fossil glen. *Nine Dragon Scroll* evening above Lake Erie. The forest rises in music like an ancient air. Twilight priestess administers the evening, her dark splendour.

Entrance colonnade to the oak forest, microclimate of hardwood shade an aerodrome nave. Distant figures numinous through summer haze. Windy August stars drift over sighing pine trees. Pine-grove star needles. When we come it rains. Indexed by sassafras trees the grassy hills undulate with soft Miocene turbulence in the July heat. High summer. Giant bulrushes. Night herons motionless on terrapin logs. An insect alights momentarily on a stainless steel stela. Luminous dream vista.

Pipes, water mains, gas lines, the roots of houses spread under the landscape. Sandy paths. Calm, alert valley air. Distant tinkle of lawn parties beside smoky rhododendrons. Honey locusts shelter summer in their foliage well into October. Cool July day, her long, honeyed thighs slipping out of her jeans as she crouches to pee in the forest loam. Fine pale arches of her feet, the hot gush of her. March hills – secret blue drifts of snow in sheltered hollows on the northern slopes. Glacial refugia.

Redtail oak forest. Narcissistic talisman of our love. A metallic green haze between the columns of this metropolitan forest – lovers wet with lust. Ginkgo leaves. August tea roses, pink, orange & cream. The constant, almost inaudible rustling of leaf mulch on warm nights in early spring. Soil and leaves heaving in slow-motion turmoil of dew worms sliding through autumnal debris, a faint, chalky cellophane crinkling.

June empire of green, coronation of green. Aquamarine and jasper. Blue-green. Yellow-green. Green of constancy and desire. Corundum. Verdigris streaks on limestone walls.

H ot, still air. Heatwaves linger in closed rooms. Unfortunate your beauty. Disastrous your lovely salamander arms beside the restaurant patio hedge. The city is a ripple-tank of violet & orange, molten steel squeezed into the shapes of machines. The simple, rude pragmatism of size. Intolerable heat of a single desk lamp as moths gather at the window screen. River musk smell of dried algae. Luscious, earthen scent of cantaloupes and peaches in a wooden bowl on the kitchen table. Tickets till dawn. Spring twigs, their buds reptilian, as we are reptilian in our extremities. Scaled & cool the clear borders of my own partiality.

The cliffbrake fern's blue-green tenacious filigree. Niagara-on-the-Lake twinkling in the stone night. Hot July afternoon. Empty apartment buildings. An extinct river reconstituted in the meandering interior of the willow brake. The children who play there. Green tissue commotion as a praying mantis rises laboriously through the August mist under a sodium vapour lamp. Indistinct conversation of restaurant patrons leaving the patio in small groups. Giant silk moth. Unseen river sliding noiselessly behind all this.

Cool summer night. Blue midnight sky behind deserted buildings. Nostalgia steeped in its own intoxication. Empty dance pavilion beneath the summer stars. Every forest is a beckoning sensual labyrinth of lust. Radiowave rooms echoing within rooms, the hollowness of love remembered within love realized. The lonely bliss of completion. Delicious emptiness in this late summer night. After the dance a waning moon rises. We walk through empty streets past buildings filled with sleepers. Their dreams perfuse the night air.

Tonight the sky is inky black, a carbon night without a trace of blue behind the full moon. It is a deeper evening, a universe slightly more vacant than before, as if this warm darkness required a triumph of representation, as if the sky conformed to its own description in a continuous devoted hue. A single cricket calls from the grass beside the barn. Indigo summer.

Purple and grey. Metallic dust in the subway tunnels. Darkness at the interstices of the city. Burgundy on limestone. Lilacs bending in a rainy wind. University residences glowing deep yellow. The airport thundering through the night air. Wind in the Wychwood oaks. Green argon lasers flicker over Queen Street sidewalks. Dirigibles. The museum deserted on a cool night. Its air-conditioned interior simulates the evening air. Asphalt lagoons. A nightflight banks over the spreading ledges of city lights. The streets are vast crystalline networks, linked luminescent organisms proliferating to the horizon. Cooling lava glowing through a lacework of cracks. Moonlight on Lake Ontario is a dazzling path to the dawn. Night corrupt of another. Slim curve of her waist unfolds itself in silence and without witness.

F ireworks explode in the summer night. Pyrotechnic blossoms of silver and gold. Their dazzling, empty perfection. Spring aches within a palace deep inside the autumn forest. A clear evening with celestial gauze so that the largest stars have misty haloes. This lucid haze signifying magic, charmed darkness. Jupiter, Mars & Venus. I know you are love, in the absorbent summer twilight of the forest strand.

Enigmatic nocturnal waves phosphoresce on the moonlit shore of an inland ocean. Beech trunks incarnate with cloud light, as if you weren't sure you were naked in a dream. Moccasin flowers. Trilliums. Lightning blossoming in the purple strata of distant storms. Wild grapevines spill from the branches of white oaks overhanging the creek. A suffusion of emerald light through the waist-high ferns, our clothes soaked with rain & sweat.

We follow the river down the Escarpment ravine. The clouds are a violet-grey ceiling to this vast, open-air greenhouse. The air thick and hot, the foliage dripping with recent rain & illuminated evenly. In the forest a deserted building witnesses our opaque Logos, the tiny furious engine of a hoverfly suspended in mid-air. Pale rain on the pond's surface. Pillars toppled by sycamores. English ivy growing behind storm windows, leaves pressed green against the glass. Darting & hovering, a flock of cedar waxwings hunts insects at the edge of the marsh.

There is a darkness outside the city. Her face vigilant through night elm corridors. Summer lawn under green cumulus trees. The city park full of couples. She resembles herself darkly, like a sensual memory. Her wrists exalting with such cruel delicacy as always attends on beauty. Our hands alive to each other. Exist, to quicken the air around us, for this moment we are golden. Red oaks. The night guides us. It is warm outside and the air moves the leaves variously. Her pelvis vaulted light. Powdery with stars from a desert night, the wind has come to blow away what is weightless in us.

D actyl leaves of the white oak. The white-tailed deer are melanized thermograms of themselves. There is a consensual domain in the summer wasteland. Giant Haida eyes stare from beech trunks, their rapt bliss.

Lyrical monotony of the whip-poor-will's song. Jupiter and Mars bright through the lattice of the oak canopy. A nightjar's haunted clockwork call conjures memories and floating reminiscences. Hollow music, as if the soul were a cuttlebone. Sinister to be so bold. Cool mist over the river. The whip-poor-will stops the night.

Multifoliate her orgasms curl and vanish into the landscape. Electric gradients motionless in the stadium heat-zone of her touching. One pure, interlocking network of desire. Thought impulses and thunder, my fingers water dispersing porous into the land. Dwarf chinquapin savannah of the Pinery dunes. Black oak. A late cold spell decelerates the unfolding spring foliage. Magnolia flowers transfixed in perpetual blossom for two weeks. Lilac and forsythia suspended in cool vegetative orgasm. Raw spring sun on tombstones. Granular luminescence in the grass.

Naked, she places her foot on a limestone boulder and reaches up into the leaves. Rapture. And touching you my dreams lay waste the foliage of your nervous system. Soft electronic hiss of night wind in the treetops. Purple night of city rain. Luminescent video-jelly oozes drugged & cool from a slice in the television cable – clear iridescent gum flickering with electric colours. The rasping call of nighthawks through an open window. Raccoon eyes glowing red in our headlights. Leaf shadows.

Delicate precision of an albino fox. Its white fur ruffled by the cool wind before the storm. Umbrella magnolia leaves amplify the sound of the first raindrops. Cold-cream scent of linden blossoms in early July. The eyespots of the polyphemus moth are reminiscent of an earlier civilization, of smooth futurist caterpillars. Their hallucinogenic blue evening reverie both alien and unconscious of itself. Large moth flower of moody smoky eyespots – rings on fawn and pink sand dunes background silent to this kingdom's maze. On the outskirts of the city there is a forest.

A muddy river shines quietly in the darkness beneath the span. Rain falling all night. Red cedars luminous with hundreds of green diamonds in the flashlight beam. The Bouguereau August light. Local time anomaly, thrilling August mist over several days. Darkness so the night can see. Waxy green gloss of oak leaves in July sun. The forest rejoices in the sound of distant waves. This choice conceived by her witnessing.

T eetering flight of a butterfly, its destination barely a probability. Dwarf hackberry. Swamp white oak. Hoary bats tumble like acrobats through the savannah airspace. Margin of evening, an indeterminate limen between creatures diurnal and nocturnal. Twilight congeals as the first raccoons descend the chinquapin oak. Hanging gardens, ceaselessly dark at the bottom where grub-jewels glisten in the hollow oak's loam.

On the grassy flats behind the dunes giant cicada-killer wasps establish restless, uneasy field colonies. Their magnetic, zigzagging, hovering flight, as if suspended on the wobbling tips of fine metal rods. Small onthophagus scarab beetles hunt for dung in the solar furnace of the Pinery dunes. Shagbark hickory and sycamore. Lights twinkling on Kettle Point at night, the long curve of the beach. Grand Bend on the Ausable. August fireflies beside the evening river, wandering fairy-lights.

The machinery stands poised and glistening in the forest clearing. The first cicadas of morning, their slow metallic grind. August rising through the fields and forests, the height of summer. The dust on the path is inlaid with a palimpsest of shoe-tread geometries in a hieroglyphic pastiche. We articulate every surface with our insignia. This internal summer a tender flood. Spiders are sinister optimists. Red bats careen through the light-cones of street lamps, their velocity gathered outside the light's perimeter.

Late August gold, silvery haze & hot wind in distant trees. Waves of wind in the grass, orange sunlight and a

black swallowtail butterfly. Goldenrod. The field
autumnal, dry. Limestone wind, damp & humid. August
where it was named. August where it began.

All the invisible cameras shift into our eyes. Deep in the
light field of the city a pink electric sky glows through
the evening foliage. Delicate rustling static of leaves
moving in the wind. Them. Honey to the quick. Spent
hurricanes of late summer, flooded culverts and
hollows. Giant sphinx moth at the porch light on a
cool evening. Black shadows beneath the white oak.
These successions swarming through the trees of the
broken consort, their branches bending in the nocturnal
heat storm.

White sunlight, white sand. All day in the dunes, leaves
of small cottonwoods on the beach wagging in a hot
lake wind. Calm bowls of still air behind the sandhills.
Tactile revelation of stone bridges the dream city.

E arly June evening. Dark overcast sky behind green
leaves. Sexual green, handsome green. Malachite.
This summer grey and startled. Our broken lives
illuminate it with such sad delight. The world is
ourselves come to this childhood wisdom.

The flesh of the apple is a strategy, the summer night
sky a cathedral of stars. In the coal swamp the
lepidodendron trees rise. Their helical blazonry of
mysterious bituminous crystal. Jet coal. Methane from
an ancient swamp suffuses the depths of a coal mine.
Giant salamanders stir in the slurry at the bottom of the
elevator shaft.

Twilight deepens as the sky loads its nightware. Bright
tedium of the whip-poor-will's call. Its empty, lonely
song is a kind of memory entrapment. This night
connected to all nights. The whip-poor-will's bubbling
call recedes into darkness. Its carnal song is an ominous
invitation, an absent counterpoint over the bleak,
modulated surge of distant diesel engines.

She is darkness enthroned, slender stem of pink mist.
Her delicate white metallic night. The summer sun low
and softly stabbing the weird music of the stars. I have
seen this day from the other side of my life. Pale, dusty
green leaves of the silver maple bending in the wind.
This wind, this light. All alone in the dream of night.
Arkona. The sound of a far horn. Unknowable desire,
unknowable wisdom. A white subtropical forest
hanging in the air like a cipher of sound. Wind
gusting on a hot afternoon.

Limestone boulders rise from the depths of the hills, eroding into fantastic shapes as they surface. The soil is an ocean, a fluid heavy with thousand-year viscosity. Blind worm snakes. Tunnels, roots, and the smooth, underground shapes of truffles. Mozart from an open window in a country home. Empty heraldry all the more profound because it is unconscious. Sitar monotone of high-tension wires humming above the transformer station. Cool May nights before the nighthawks arrive. She is otherworldly, immediate.

Sunspots crackle through the radio waves. The planets are caught in that higher music. Aurora borealis. Solar wind conjures an iridescent crown on top of the world. Sweet nocturnal fragrance of sycamore foliage. Silver stars cast into the dark wells of the sky. The wind a waterfall in the treetops. The marvellous machines wait silently in the forest clearing, starlight gleaming on their polished metal contours. Mood palaces deep within an oak tree. Smoke tendrils rise from the smouldering campfire, time unfolds in arabesques.

S weet desert of soul spreading into the city you *are* this still evening. Andromeda galaxy overhead, a tiny, fuzzy colossus. The night sky a time-mosaic. Distant symphonies from the bandshell in the park. Eocene light, Mesozoic light, light from before the earth existed. Time wind blowing through the Milky Way. An evanescent stardust settles on the flowers in the garden.

The night sky is prehistory factored by the speed of light, a thick lens of time jelly, photon molasses. The faintest stars further back in time the edge of the universe is its beginning. The pure retrospection of starlight, lamented light from extinct suns and distant galaxies. Countless stars that have shone on forgotten cultures of unknowable complexity. Lost technologies in the hard silver twinkle at the edge of this pond.

A gold scarab waits within the cottage dream. Clark Point. In the river the green newts are resting, still and random, strewn by gnostic impulse in the sandy shallows. Beside them miniature underwater mountainscapes of algae and pond weed. A scarlet tanager flies through the green oaks. Limestone pavement showing bare through patches in the savannah. Moonlight deep inside a dark October lake. Our strange, liquid intimacy in this lush landscape. Thrill of moist warm air in secret rooms the velvet light. Sex a delicious conspiracy focusing the wisdom of the trees.

Clarion fountain above all this. Jazz saxophone sliding languid over the pool in smoky loops and tusks. Hypnotic music of desire. The logic of indiscretion. Soft-shelled terrapins slip into the water at our approach. Late April storm and lightning-sparkle saturates our peripheral vision until our flesh flickers. We make love in the rush of warm rain. Orgasm-shivers flash neuronal like foxfire through our single body. Thunder rupturing the clouds overhead in wild, extraneous, baritone ventriloquism. The rain splashing on your long thighs. Goosebumps, rain foam pubic hair, dangling come jelly we make love on our knees. Thunder rippling above, murmuring like memory or revenge. The grassfires of early April. Fortnight of dry weather before the foliage humidity engages.

There is only one night, one day. The March full moon the last high, winter moon. In April the lunar arc is low in the southern sky, a summer moon.

Outdoor concert in the park bandshell. The empty stage is lit. The audience is a dark mammalian cobble of heads extending into darkness beyond the footlights. Above the stage the stars are shining. In summer our afternoons are bright and cruel with youth. These our mouths, our sex, are dark openings into mute unknowable bliss. As if the city were a desert and we were a people of prophecy. Spring on the Forbidden Planet, dune reverie of lost alien civilizations. Blades of grass are narrow, supplicating astronomers in the night wind. Realm sensualist her gold mail and silk indispensable. Midnight dew trickles down the sides of the glass machinery.

The afternoon we fell through each other into this magnificent autumn of fire and ice. We haunt this season in a white room, flickering ultraviolet light flooding insubstantial through the architecture of our skin. You are a leaf drifting to earth, a thin, spiral galaxy. This sunny autumn wind. The blue optical spruce. You are worshipped in the emptiness at the threshold of the temple.

S pring insists, in its tragic splendour. Crickets
interrogate the night, their insect Morse a
sourceless gamelan. Still summer evening, pink-gold
sunset over the viaduct trestles. Wish now the train
were upon us. Ultraviolet moon in a purple sky.
Together we are erotic technicians. The exquisite panic
of orgasm, divine rush of electric honey flesh burning
the mind clear. The immanent hush of pure existence,
rapture in the grey 1911 industrial Victorian landscape.
Iroquois delirium of the sandy red tobacco fields near
Delhi. The Milky Way a dusty star trail high over the
Huron dunes.

Middle Island. Sandusky, Ohio. Neutral rimsherds
catch the evening sun on the forest floor. This site
continuously inhabited since the mammoths. Smooth,
low-grade ecstasy of summer evenings – soon giant
moths and shining chestnut-coloured beetles. Tornado
music drifting up the Thames valley from Windsor.
Spencer Davis Group faintly on the windy radio
tonight. Morning mist over the lily pads, zebra
swallowtails weave pointillist diagonal nets above the
milkweed blossoms.

Sitar drone of cicadas in the understorey of the
coppice, hills covered with young hardwoods. Brief
stroboscopic flicker of a bird passing overhead.
Pathless living-room forest of trunks, leaf-litter
and patches of sunlight beneath the leaves.
Vultures ride hot thermals above the crest of the
Escarpment.

Late nineteen-sixties basement rec room, wood-panelled summer trapped in the cool, windy September night forest. Summer with walls, summer interiorized by coolness and finiteness – intimate, desperate summer. The faint scent of skunk. Summer self-confident and mortal riding maximal the dreams of September. Summer like gimmick mountain. Synthetic, autumnal summer.

Lust under the industrial floodlights. Aromatic with new leaves and warm soil the night sky is a cavern filled with stars. Dark emerald wind blowing through the trees. We walk under the constellations out onto the lawn. Oak Ridge Moraine conceives ravines to the north. Layers of brown lignite with lenses of carbonized peat. Glassy vugs filled with anthracite crystals. Hibernating lungfish sleeping in their dried mucus sacs. Their 300-million-year exile.

In the twilight a giant sphinx hawkmoth hovers among the nicotinia flowers, its long, wiry tongue glinting in the streetlight as it threads the necks of the blossoms. Distant traffic on the Lakeshore Expressway. Waning moon rising like a stained memory, a maculate reminiscence of its fullness. The evening sunlight on these pink, finite flowers, only once – eternal in the certainty that this tableau will never be again. An infinite series of such moments, each nesting a thousand inner moments. All illuminated by the metallic, golden light.

In late March a comet effloresces at the zenith, its pale areolus like a supernumerary nipple. The comet an omen, an emissary of cool summer darkness. The eye of the comet is a soundless moaning fetish, its tail a blown phosphorescent æther, alarming smudge of infra-moonlight. Tonight the comet is an apostrophe of time hanging in the night sky while March mud congeals and freezes under the trees. The comet a tenuous continent, a presence in the stars, a vanishing spectral finger pointing with monotonous, empty grace at the sun. Such silence, such distant commotion.

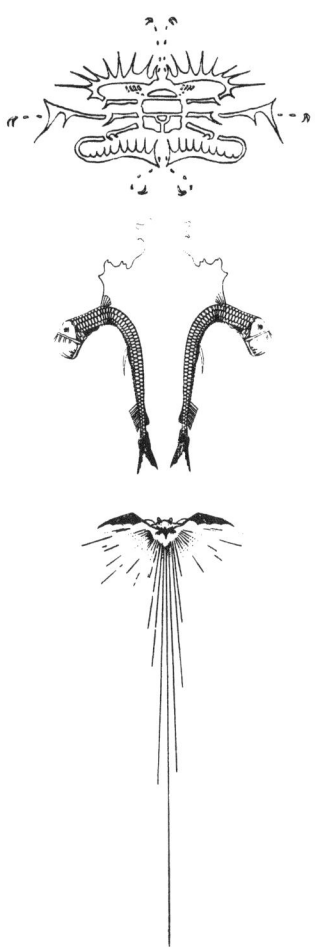

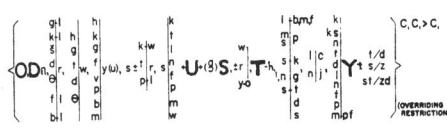

AUTHOR'S NOTE

Books III and IV of *A Natural History of Southwestern Ontario* were written between August 1981 and March 1996. "Concordat Proviso Ascendant," Book III of *A Natural History,* was published by *The Figures*, Massachusetts, as a monograph. Excerpts from "Time Wind," Book IV of *A Natural History,* have appeared in *Grand Street*, *Matrix*, and *Poetry Canada Review*. The poem "Long Tooth" appeared in the *Queen Street Quarterly*.

ACKNOWLEDGEMENTS

I thank Stan Dragland for his attentive reading of these poems; his commentary was valuable to me during the final stages of editing. I also thank Barbara Gowdy, whose ear is as finely tuned for poetry as it is for prose, and who helped me in the final preparation as well. Much thanks go to Ellen Seligman, who guided the manuscript through the publishing process and provided a friendly office. I thank Avie Bennett and Douglas Gibson, who continue to support and publish poetry. Thanks are due also to those who assisted at McClelland & Stewart: Peter Buck, Anita Chong, and Sari Ginsberg. Finally, I thank the Toronto Arts Council, the Ontario Arts Council, and the Canada Council, who all contributed to the preparation of this book.